Progressive
Around the Drums with
Syncopation

by Jim Latta

90 MINUTE STEREO
CASSETTE AVAILABLE

The most important exercises in
Progressive Around the Drums with Syncopation
have been recorded onto a 90 minute STEREO cassette
tape and will be a valuable aid to your progress.

Cassettes available from all good music stores or direct from:—

U.S.A. — $9.99
(Ca. residents add tax)
Koala Publications Inc.
3001 Redhill Ave.
Bldg. 2 # 104
Costa Mesa
CA. 92626
Ph. (714) 546 2743
Fax 1-714-546 2749

Australia — $14.95
Koala Publications Pty. Ltd.
4 Captain Cook Avenue
Flinders Park
South Australia 5025
Ph (08) 268 1750
Fax 61 8 347 4019

U.K. & Europe — £6.25
(includes V.A.T.)
Music Exchange,
Mail Order Dept.
Claverton Rd, Wythenshawe
Manchester M23 9NE
Ph (061) 946 1234
Fax (061) 946 1195

If ordering direct please add $1.00 or 50p. postage per cassette. Payment by cheque or money order.

*I dedicate this book to my wife
and best friend Pat. (The girl from Jersey)*

Acknowledgements
Cover: Phil Martin
Instruments supplied by John Reynolds Drum City

Distributed By

in **Australia**
Koala Publications
4 Captain Cook Ave.
Flinders Park 5025
South Australia
Ph (08) 268 1750
Fax (08) 347 4019

in **U.S.A.**
Koala Publications
3001 Redhill Ave.
Bldg. 2 # 104
Costa Mesa CA
U.S.A. 92626
Ph (714) 546 2743
Fax 1-714-546 2749

in **U.K. and Europe**
Music Exchange
Claverton Road, Wythenshawe,
Manchester M23 9NE
Ph (061) 946 1234
Fax (061) 946 1195

ISBN 0 947183 69 8

Reorder code KP-SD

COPYRIGHT CONDITIONS
No part of this book may be reproduced in any form without written consent from the publishers.
© **1992 Koala Publications**

Contents

Introduction 5
Explanation of Drum Notation 6
Counting Guide 7

SECTION ONE 8
Approach to Practice 8

Lesson 1 – Quarter Notes, Quarter Note Rests and Half Note Rests 9

Lesson 2 – Eighth Notes and Quarter Notes 11

Lesson 3 – Dotted Eighth Note joined to Sixteenth Note
with Quarter Notes 13

Lesson 4 – Eighth Note Triplets with Quarter Notes 15

Lesson 5 – Eighth Note Triplets with Eighth Notes 17

Lesson 6 – Eighth Note Triplets with Dotted Eighth Notes
joined to Sixteenth Notes 19

Lesson 7 – Eighth Notes with Dotted Eighth Note
joined to Sixteenth Note 21

Lesson 8 – Sixteenth Notes and Quarter Notes 23

Lesson 9 – Sixteenth Notes and Eighth Notes 25

Lesson 10 – Sixteenth Notes with Dotted Eighth Note
joined to Sixteenth Note 27

Lesson 11 – Eighth Notes joined to two Sixteenth Notes with
Eighth Notes and Sixteenth Notes 29

Lesson 12 – Eighth Note joined to two Sixteenth Notes
with Dotted Eighth Note joined to a Sixteenth Note 33

Lesson 13 – Sixteenth Note - Eighth Note - Sixteenth Note
joined as a group of three with Quarter Notes 36

Lesson 14 – Sixteenth Note - Eighth Note - Sixteenth Note
joined as a group of three with Eighth Notes 38

(Contents continued next page)

Contents (cont.)

Lesson 15 – Sixteenth Note - Eighth Note - Sixteenth Note joined as a group of three with Dotted Eighth Note joined to a Sixteenth Note 40

Lesson 16 – Sixteenth Note - Eighth Note - Sixteenth Note joined as a group of three with Sixteenth Notes 42

Lesson 17 – Sixteenth Note - Eighth Note - Sixteenth Note joined as a group of three with Eighth Note joined to two Sixteenth Notes.....44

Lesson 18 – Sixteenth Note - Eighth Note - Sixteenth Note joined as a group of three with Sixteenth Notes and Eighth Notes joined to two Sixteenth Notes 46

SECTION TWO 49

Lesson 19 – Eighth Note Rest with Eighth Notes and Quarter Notes 50

Lesson 20 – Introducing Syncopation 53
Tied Notes 58

Lesson 21 – Syncopation 60

Lesson 22 – Bass Drum Control for Basic Rhythms 66

Introduction

Progressive "Around the Drums with Syncopation" has been designed to give drummers, of all styles and levels of playing ability, a carefully graded introduction to reading and playing drum music. The drum player is introduced to basic rhythms and then gradually introduced to syncopated rhythms using the whole drum kit.

Although a drummer can enjoy a career playing certain forms of music never having to read, it can extremely limit his playing skills. By simply learning to read and play the exercises in this book your musicianship will increase dramatically.

Jim Latta M.I.M.T.
(Member, Institute of Music Teachers)

JIM LATTA
M. I. M. T.
(Member, Institute of Music Teachers)

Jim Latta is senior lecturer in Drums and Percussion at the college for Technical and further education. He has performed with many Jazz and Pop artists including Don Burrows, Bee Gees, Shirley Bassey, John Farnham, George Golla, Pete Condoli and Frank Rosolino.
    Jim also works as session musician and teacher.

Explanation of Drum Notation

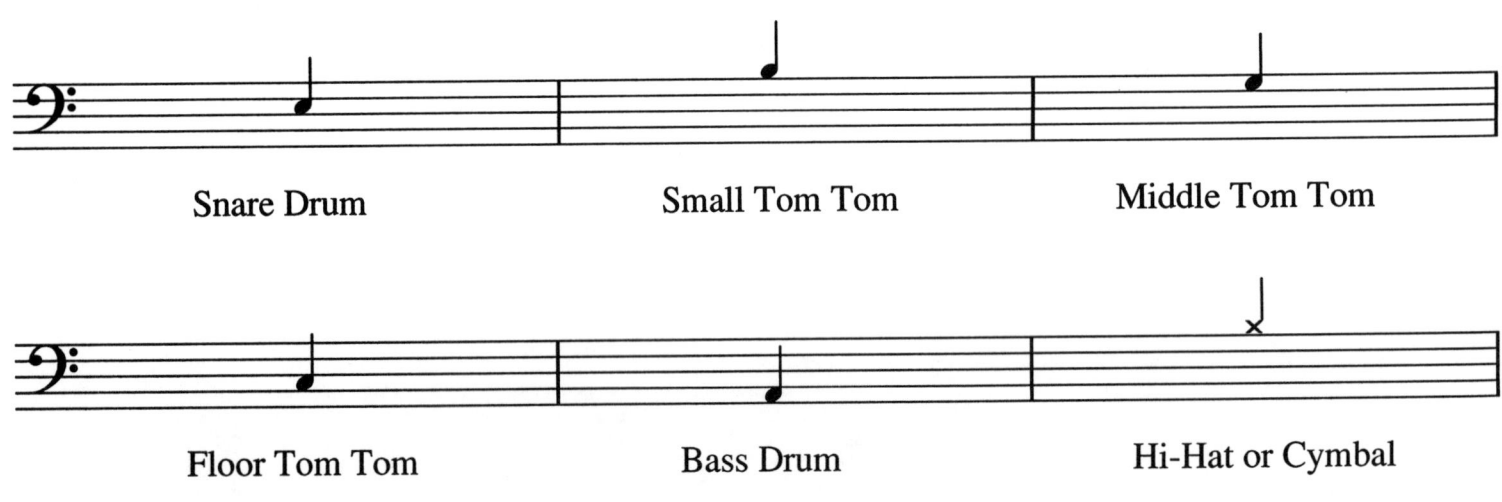

> = Accent

* Please note that stem direction is likely to alternate e.g. up ♩ or down ♩.

Counting Guide

Notes	Notation and Count	Say
Quarter Notes	♩ ♩ ♩ ♩ 1 2 3 4	one two three four
Eighth Notes	1 + 2 + 3 + 4 +	one and two and three and four and "and" is pronounced "an"
Eighth Note Triplets	1 + a 2 + a 3 + a 4 + a	one and a, two and a, three and a, four and a "a" is pronounced as "uh" Say 1 triplet, 2 triplet, 3 triplet, 4 triplet to help get the "feel" of the rhythm
Sixteenth Notes	1 e + a 2 e + a 3 e + a 4 e + a	one e and a, two e and a, three e and a, four e and a, "e" is pronounced "ee"
Eighth Note plus two Sixteenth Notes	1 e + a 2 e + a 3 e + a 4 e + a	one-and a, two-and a, three-and a, four-and a Say boom-chucka, boom-chucka to help get the "feel" of the rhythm
Two Sixteenth Notes plus an Eighth Note	1 e + a 2 e + a 3 e + a 4 e + a	one e and, two e and, three e and, four e and Say chucka-boom, chucka-boom, to help get the "feel" of the rhythm
Dotted Eighth Notes plus a Sixteenth Note	1 e + a 2 e + a 3 e + a 4 e + a	one-a, two-a, three-a, four-a
Sixteenth Note plus Eighth Note plus a Sixteenth Note	1 e + a 2 e + a 3 e + a 4 e + a	one e-a, 2 e-a, 3 e-a, 4 e-a e-a pronounced "ee-uh".

Section One

The 15 Lessons in Section One use basic notation rhythms around the drums. Incorporating quarter notes, eighth notes, sixteenth notes, triplets, dotted eighth notes and combinations of each.

Approach to Practice

It is important to have a correct approach to practice. You will benefit more from several short practices e.g. 30-40 mins every day rather than one or two long sessions per week. Work your way through this book exercise by exercise. Try to read and count (aloud) each exercise, don't just play them from memory. It is very important to be able to count each exercise. If you can't count them correctly you will not be able to play them correctly. Use alternate sticking at first then use your own. Practice slowly at first and increase speed as your reading and playing ability improves. To ensure you play each rhythm correctly the audio cassette containing the exercises is highly recommended, as is the guidance of an experienced teacher.

Refer to the counting guide on the previous page before commencing each lesson.

16 Bar Solo Exercise

Lesson 2

Eighth Notes (♫) and Quarter Notes (♩)

16 Bar Solo Exercise

Lesson 3

Dotted Eighth Note joined to Sixteenth Note (♪.♬) with Quarter Notes (♩)

16 Bar Solo Exercise

Lesson 4

16 Bar Solo Exercise

16 Bar Solo Exercise

16 Bar Solo Exercise

Lesson 7

16 Bar Solo Exercise

Lesson 8

16 Bar Solo Exercise

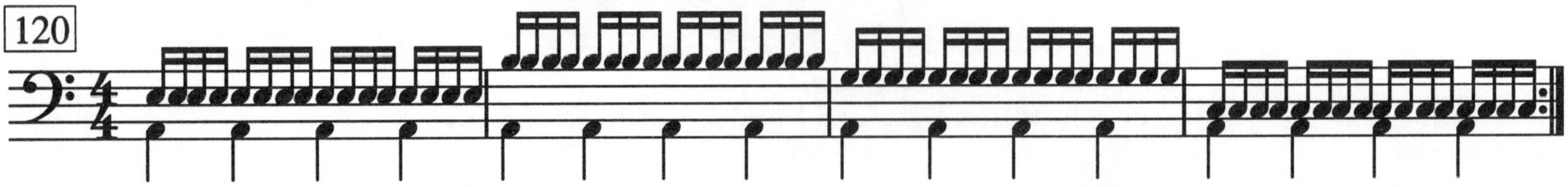

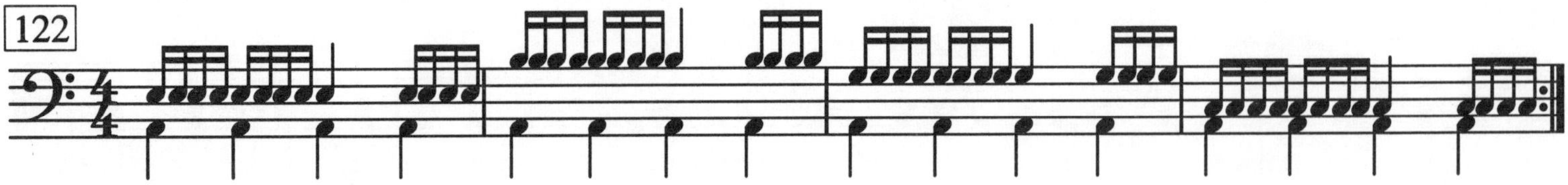

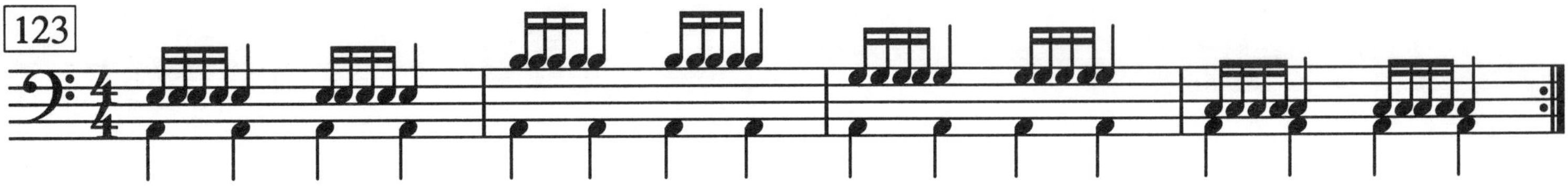

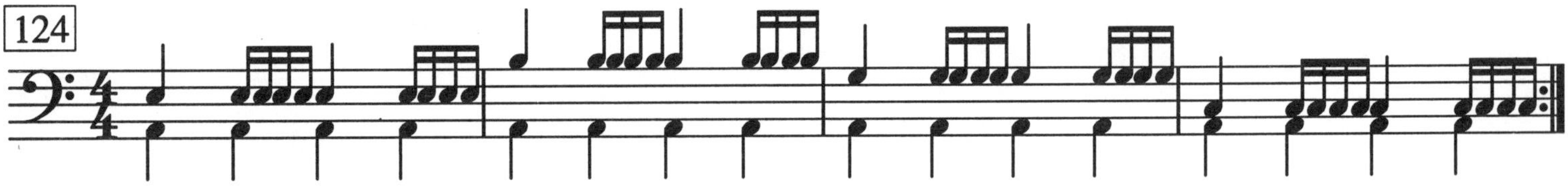

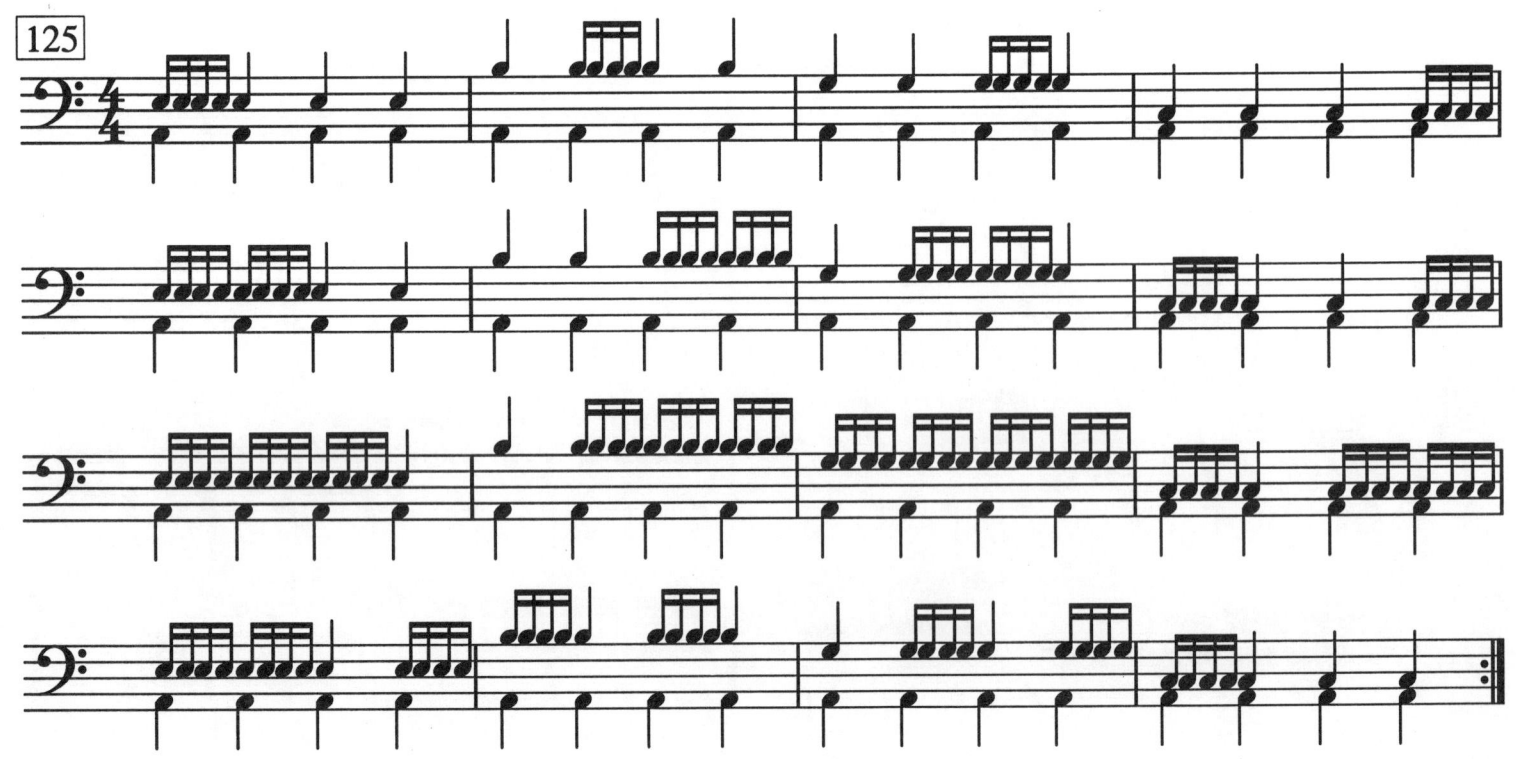

16 Bar Solo Exercise

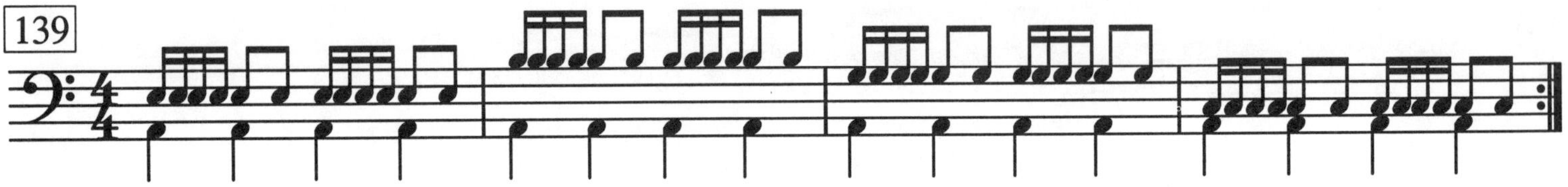

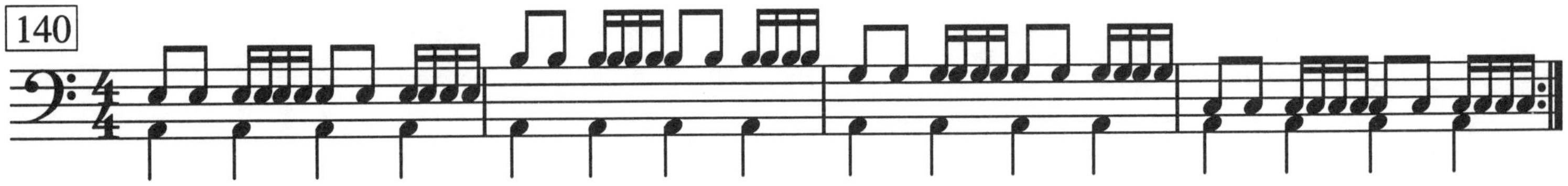

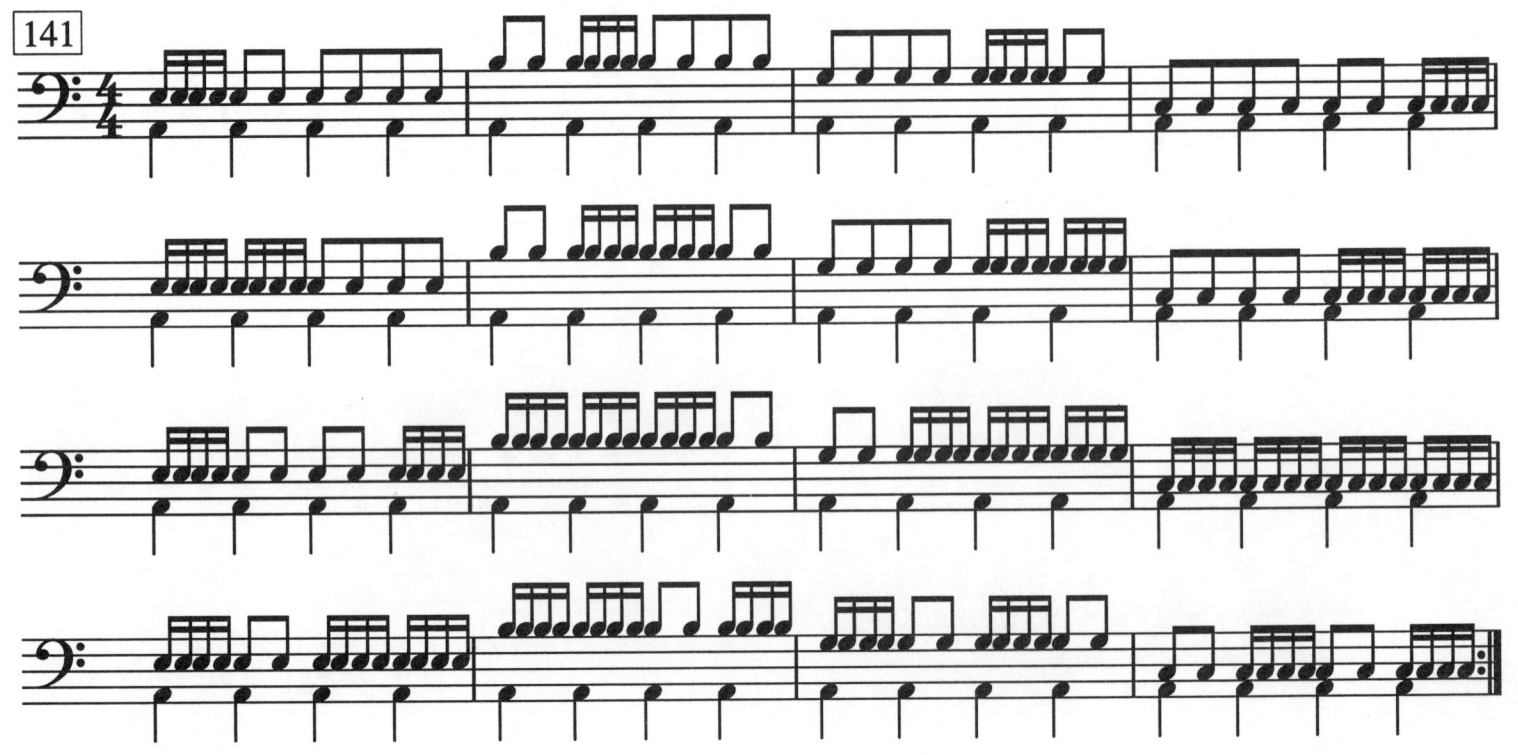

Stick Control — By George Lawrence Stone
Independence, Stick Control & Basic Reading

Around The Drums With Syncopation — By Jim Latta
Develop basic reading skills — Available @ merchandise table

The New Breed — By Gary Chester
Independence & Reading (not for beginners) — Modern Drummer Publication

2\3 or not 2\3 — By Efrain Toro
Afro-Cuban Grooves for Bass & Drums — By Lincoln Goines & Robbie Ameen
Comes w\ CD or Cassette
Afro-Cuban Rhythms for Drumset — By Frank Malabe & Bob Weiner
Comes w\ CD or Cassette
All these help to teach Latin styles & are great for independence

Advanced Funk Studies — By Rick Latham
Linear reading & independence

Syncopation for All — By Jake Hanna
Big Band Style figures for advanced readers

For Hands Only — By Efrain Toro
Developing Hand Drumming technique (for advanced readers)

← thru in L.A.

Lesson 10

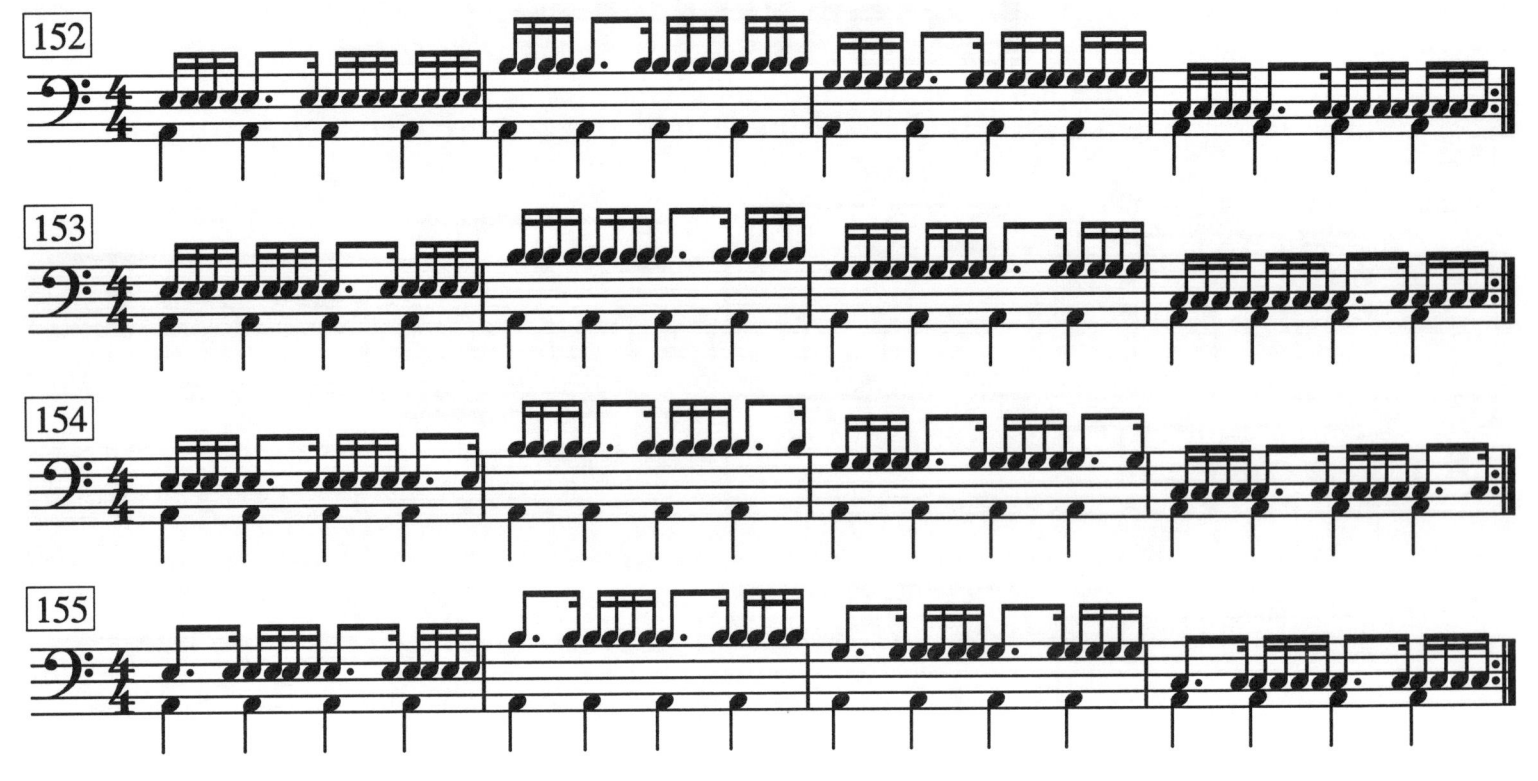

16 Bar Solo Exercise

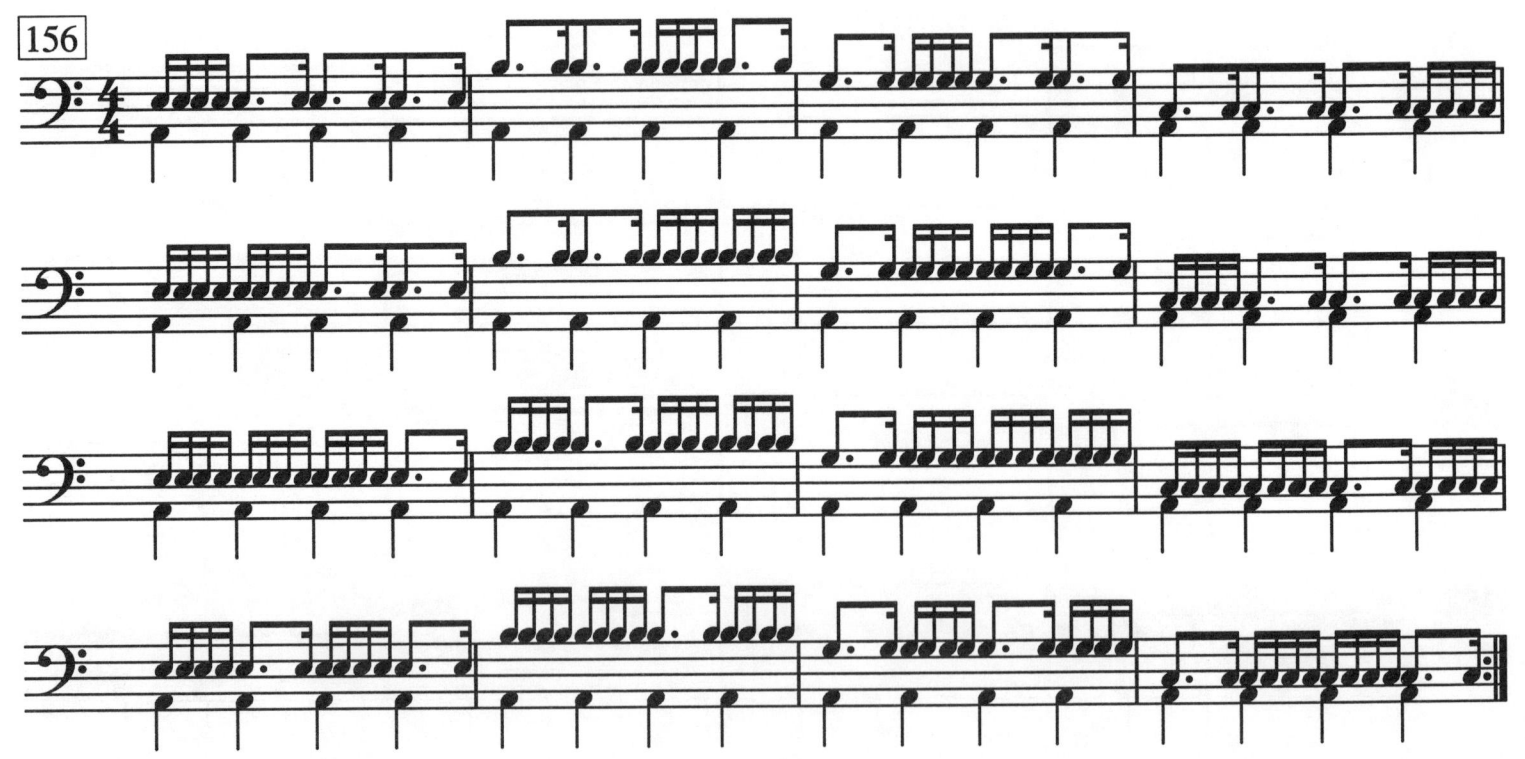

Lesson 11

32 Bar Solo Exercise

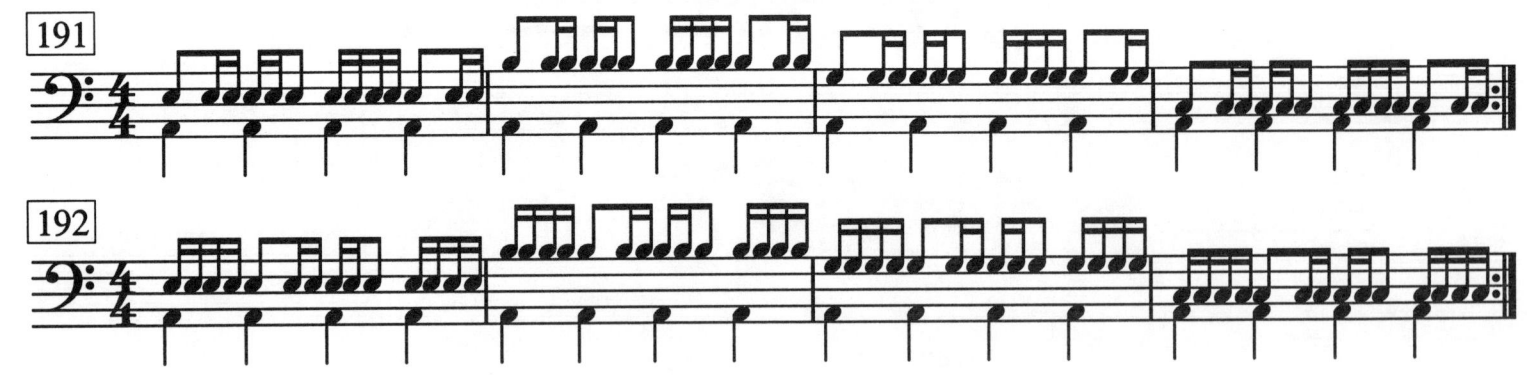

34

16 Bar Solo Exercise

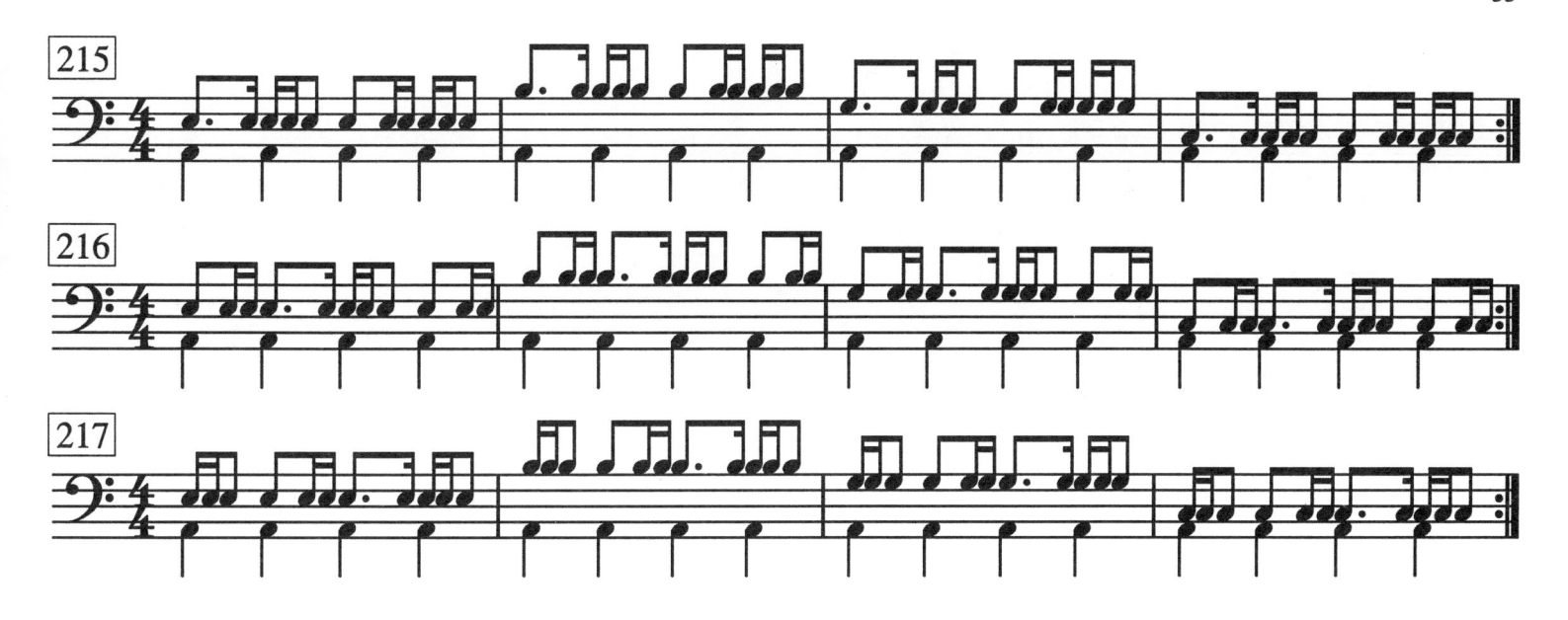

Lesson 13

Sixteenth Note - Eighth Note – Sixteenth Note joined as a group of three with Quarter Notes

16 Bar Solo Exercise

Lesson 14

Sixteenth Note - Eighth Note – Sixteenth Note joined as a group of three (♬♪) with Eighth Notes (♪♪)

16 Bar Solo Exercise

Lesson 15

Sixteenth Note – Eighth Note – Sixteenth Note joined as a group of three
with Dotted Eighth Note joined to a Sixteenth Note

16 Bar Solo Exercise

Lesson 16

Sixteenth Note - Eighth Note – Sixteenth Note joined as a group of three (♬♩) with Sixteenth Notes (♬♬)

16 Bar Solo Exercise

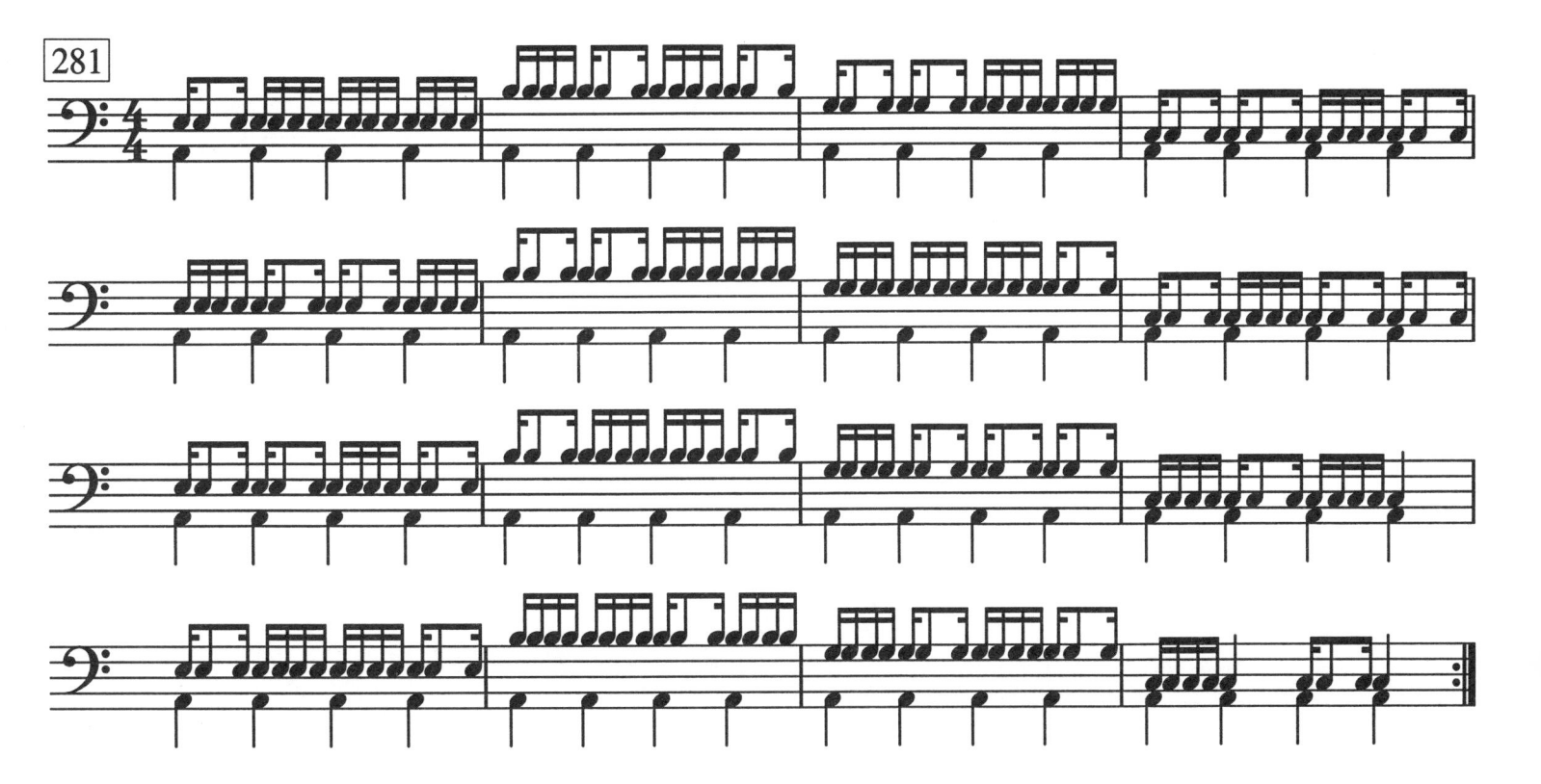

Lesson 17

Sixteenth Note – Eighth Note – Sixteenth Note joined as a group of three (♫)
with Eighth Note joined to two Sixteenth Notes (♪♫ and ♫♪)

16 Bar Solo Exercise

Lesson 18

46

Sixteenth Note – Eighth Note – Sixteenth Note joined as a group of three (♫) with Sixteenth Notes (♬) and Eighth Notes joined to two Sixteenth Notes (♪♫ and ♫♪) etc.

16 Bar Solo Exercise

32 Bar Solo Exercise

Incorporating all Exercises from Lessons Ten to Fourteen.

Section Two

The four remaining lessons in Section Two introduce basic syncopation around the drums, incorporating eighth note rests, with eighth notes, quarter notes and tied notes.

When practicing these exercises, always start *slowly* and *count* (out loud if necessary) keeping a steady even pulse with the bass drum.

The last pages in Section Two are exercises specifically designed for bass drum control. Reliable foot control is essential and these exercises will help considerably.

Lesson 19

Eighth Note Rest (𝄾) with Eighth Notes (♫) and Quarter Notes (♩)

327

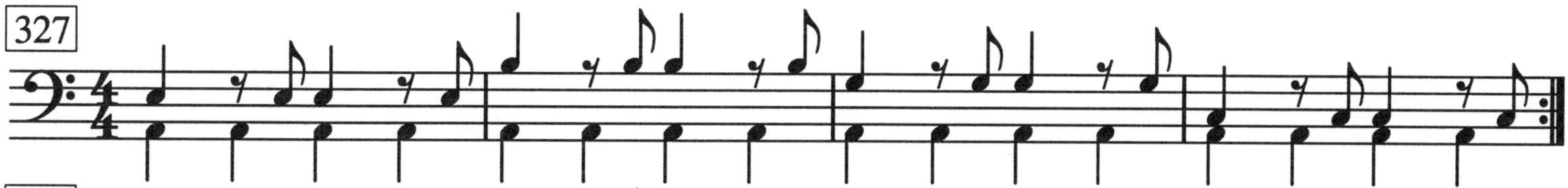

328

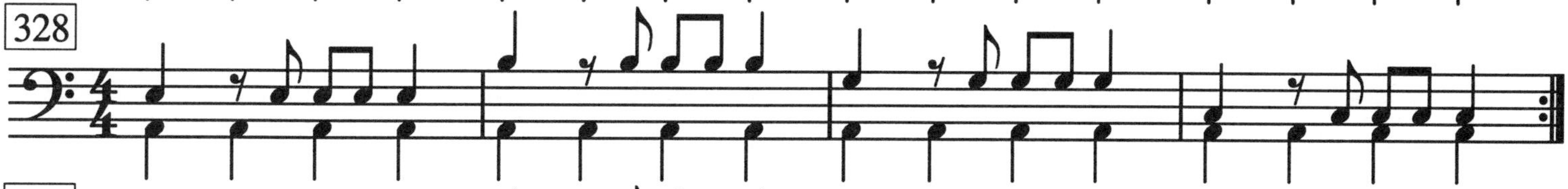

329

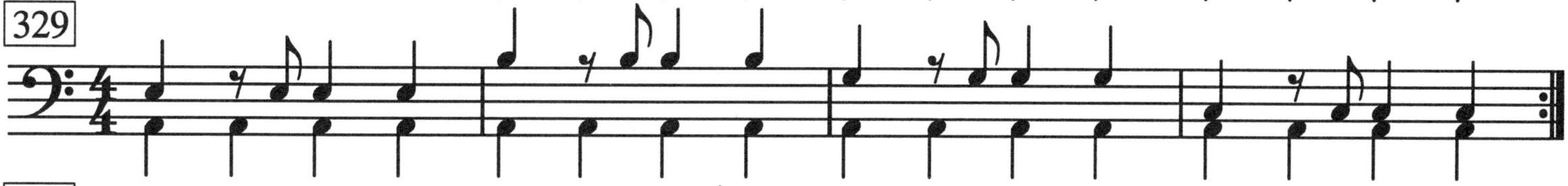

330

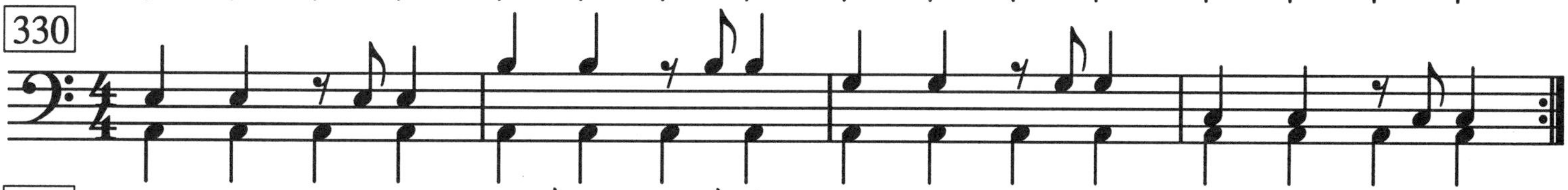

331

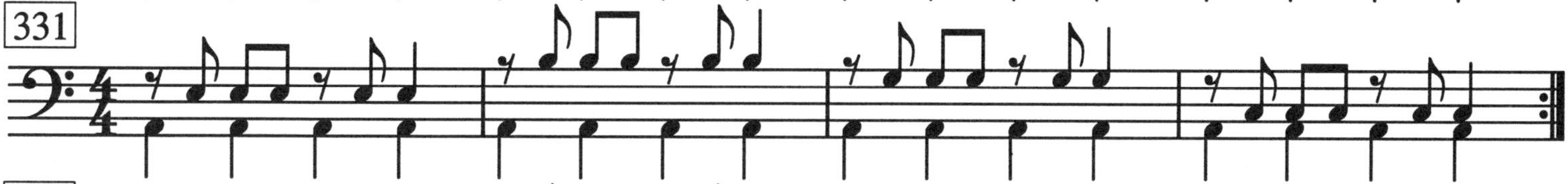

332

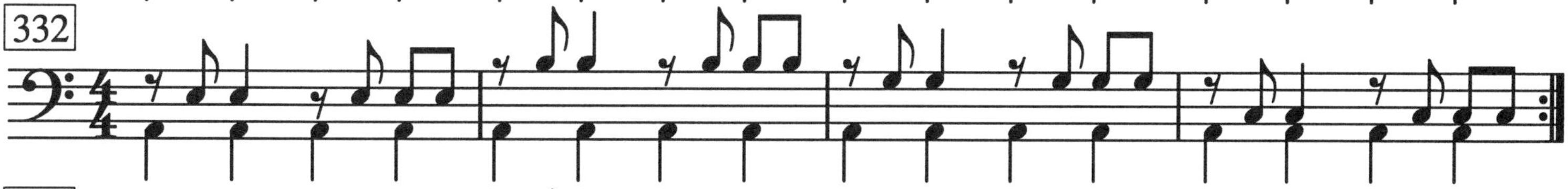

333

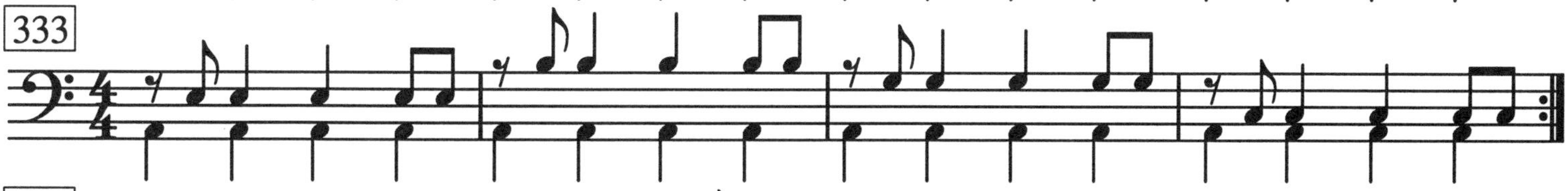

334

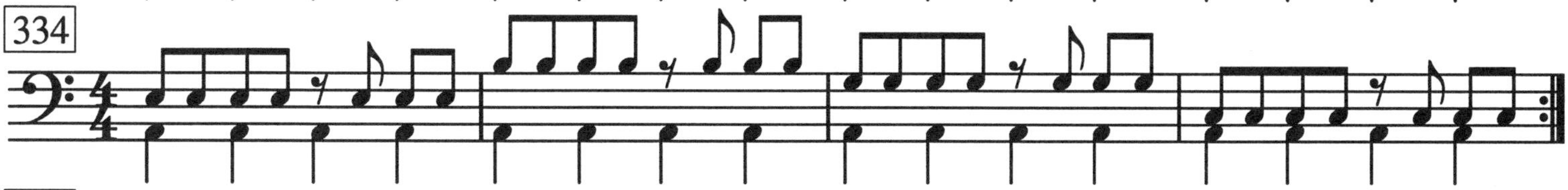

335

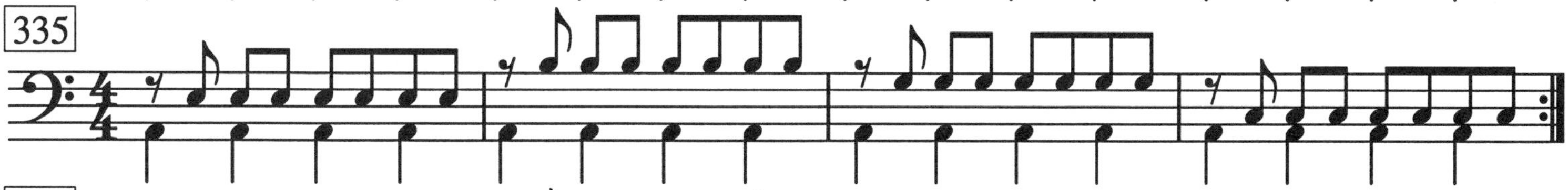

336

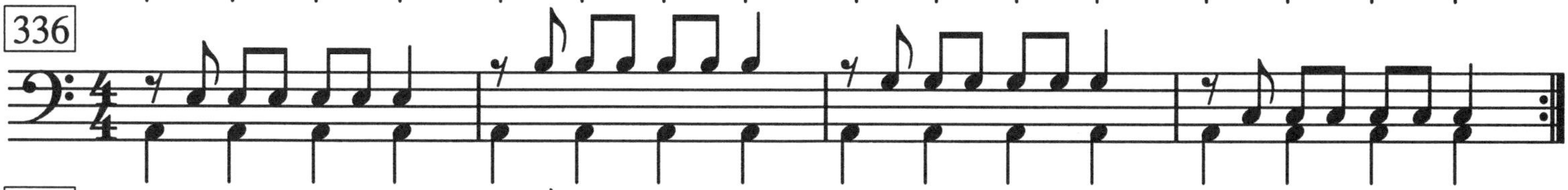

337

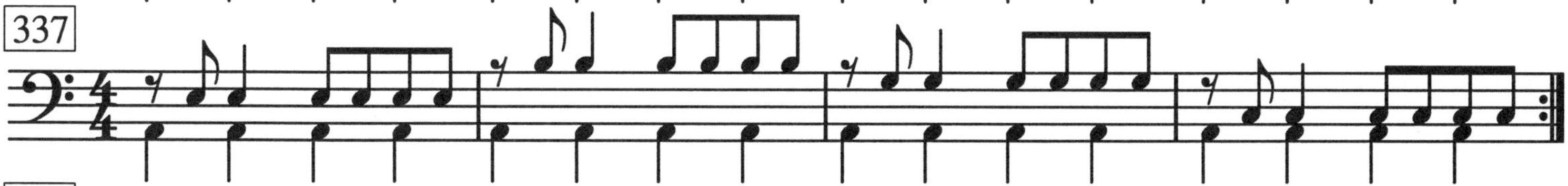

338

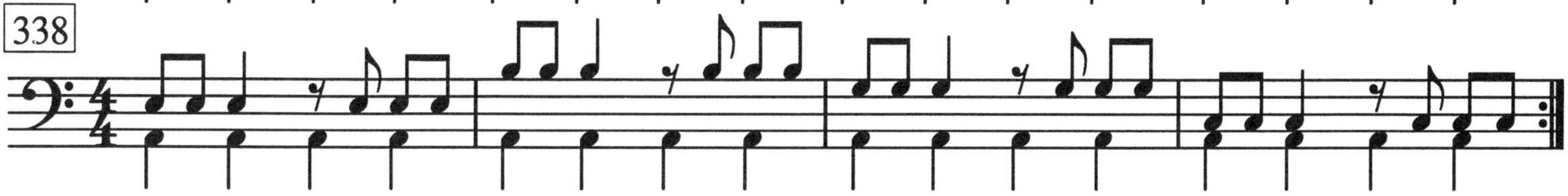

32 Bar Solo Exercise

Lesson 20
Introducing Syncopation

Syncopation is the accenting of a normally unaccented beat. i.e. an "off the beat" rhythm.

e.g. a basic rhythm

a syncopated rhythm

The key to learning how to read syncopation is to learn how to **count** it correctly. Drummers more than any other instrumentalist seem to have a problem with this. Part of the reason is that few books offer drummers a complete explanation, especially for beginners.

We commence with a study of 8 eighth notes and the way they are **counted**, which is:

Counted: "and" "and" "and" "and"
            1 + 2 + 3 + 4 +

For simplification, we will refer to this as Key Number One.

Divide a bar of $\frac{4}{4}$ time into eight eighth notes.

Count 1 + 2 + 3 + 4 +

There are two eighth notes in a quarter note.
So a quarter note could be

♩ =(1+) or (2+) or (3+) or (4+)

or   ♩ = (+2) or (+3) or (+4) section of the count

An eighth note can be

♪ = (1) or (2) or (3) or (4)

or any of the "ands" (+)

A dotted note is equal to three notes half its value e.g. ♩. = ♪♪♪

Therefore a dotted quarter note (♩.) is equal to three eighth notes.

♩. = (1+2) or (+2+) or (2+3) or (+3+) or (3+4) or (+4+) section of the count.

If you wish to work out a bar of syncopation, for example: 4/4 ♪ ♩ ♩ ♩ ♪ | place it under the "key" like so:

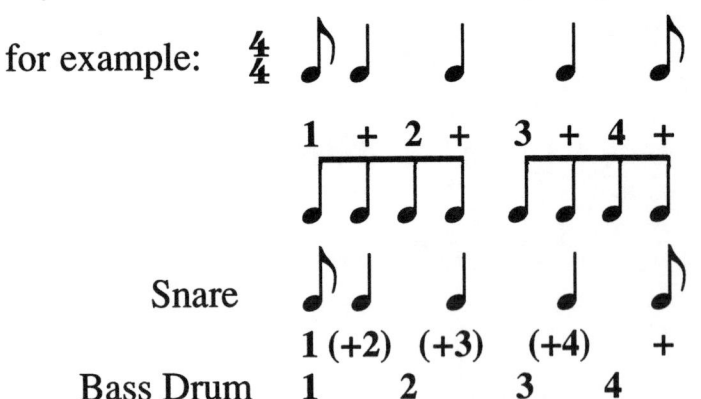

```
1  +  2  +   3  +  4  +
♪♪♪♪        ♪♪♪♪

Snare        ♪ ♩   ♩    ♩   ♪
             1 (+2) (+3) (+4)  +
Bass Drum    1   2    3    4
```

Play the bass drum on all the numbers, as a time keeper. Count out loud "**1+2+3+4+**" and play the syncopated beat.

Because of the characteristic of the instrument, drummers cannot "hang on" to a note, or play much longer than a quarter note (unless a closed roll [buzz roll] or cymbal crash is played). As a result of this, drummers may be required to read **three** ways of playing the same drum pattern.

In the 12 exercises on page 55, each bar, although written differently, sounds the same when played by a drummer.

The middle bar of each exercise incorporates tied notes. The second note of a tie is not played.

e.g. written as ♩ ♩ ♩ (tied)   played as ♩ ♩ 𝄽

Note: The bass drum is deleted on these exercises so you can see how the syncopation is counted without the aid of a **written** bass drum.

Use page 55 as a guide, especially for the exercises on syncopation where the bass drum has been deleted.

Study this page carefully.
Note the **three** ways of writing the same pattern.
(For tied notes – refer page 58).

Play the following examples of syncopation around the drums.
Bass drum keeps a steady beat.

Count 1 + 2 + 3 4 etc.

364

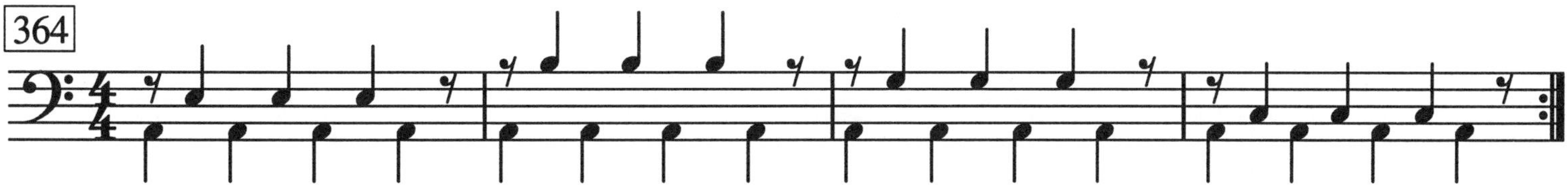

365

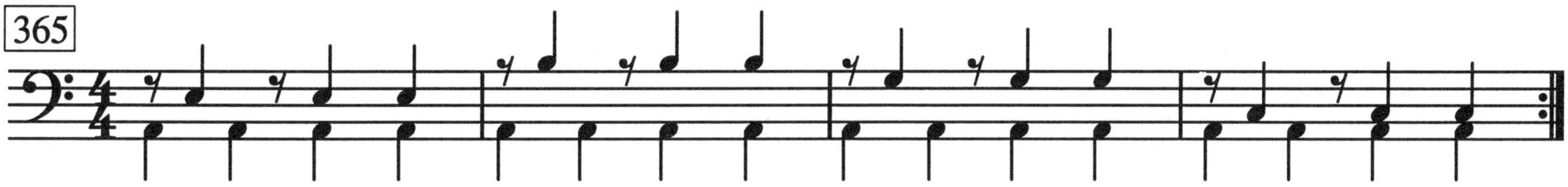

366

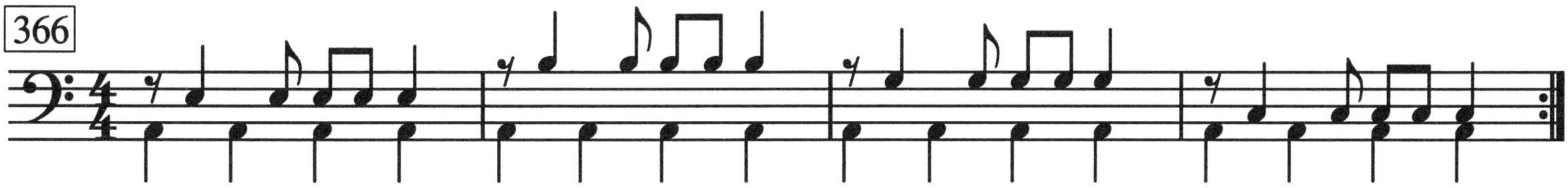

367

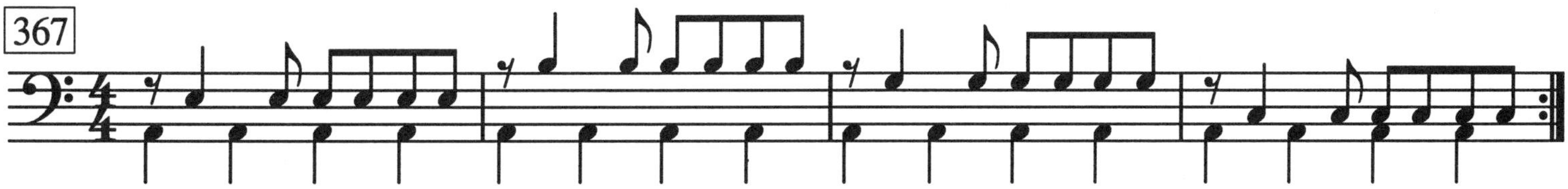

368

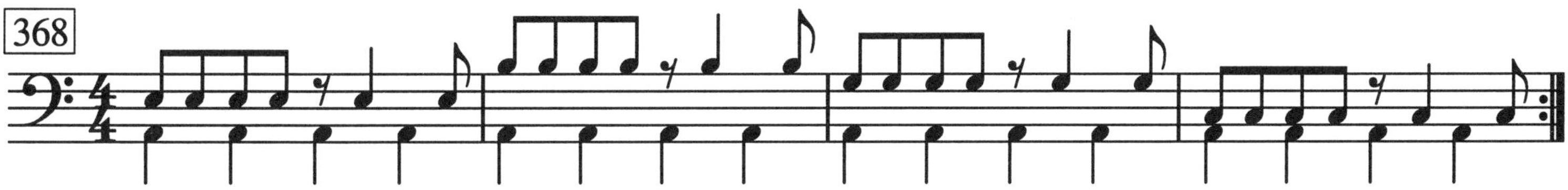

369

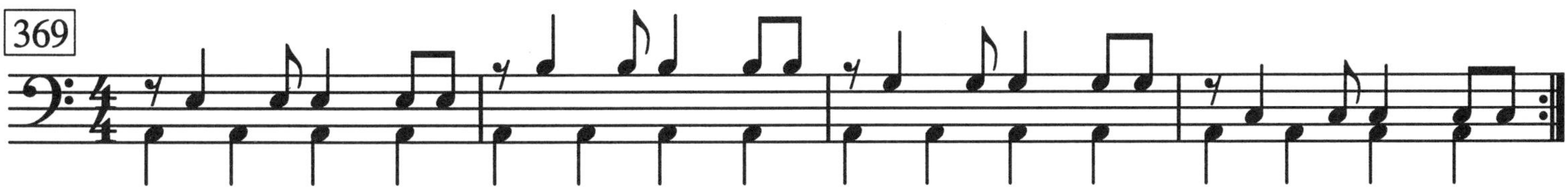

370

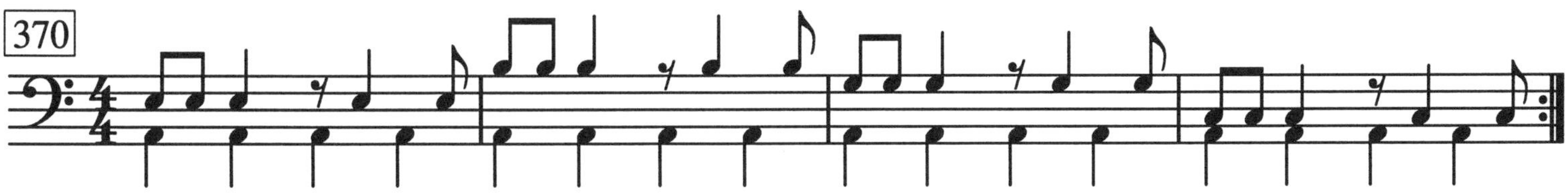

371

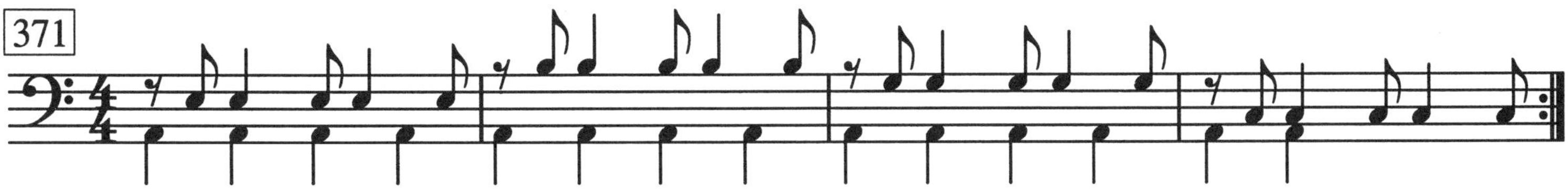

Tied Notes

Because drummers cannot always hold a note to its correct value, as most other instruments can, it is essential for beginners to treat the **second** note of the tie as a rest, and not to play it.
Here are some examples:

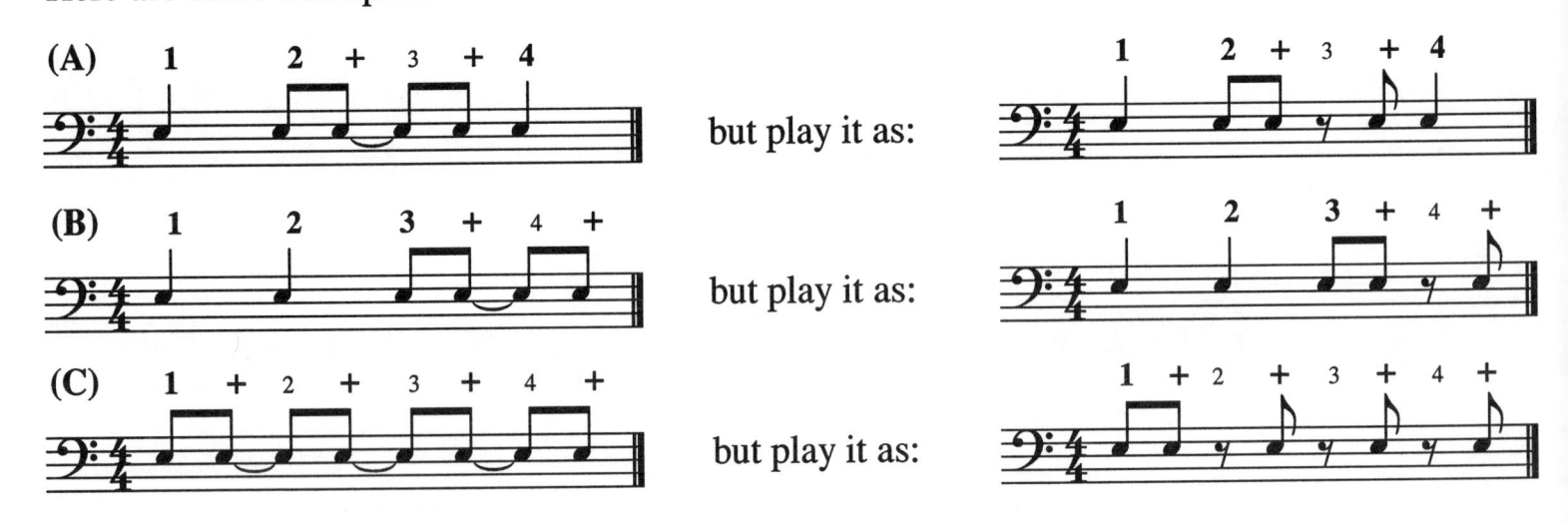

(A)

but play it as:
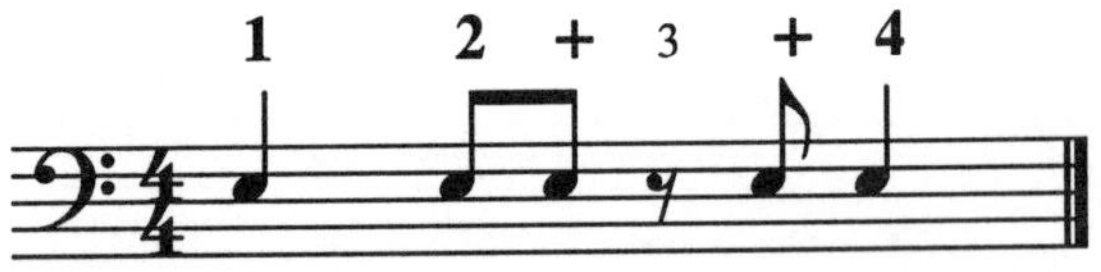

(B)

but play it as:

(C)

but play it as:

In Example (A) think of the 1st half of the 3rd beat as a rest. In Example (B) think of the 1st half of the 4th beat as a rest. In Example (C) think of the 1st half of beats 2, 3, 4 as rests.

372

373

374

375

376

377

378

24 Bar Solo Exercise

Lesson 21

Syncopation

The bass drum plays a steady 4 beats per bar (although not written). This helps you to read syncopation more effectively. The following exercises are on snare only.

32 Bar Solo Exercise

Play slowly - count aloud - alternate sticking.

Once you have completed playing exercises 354 - 385 as written go back and play them as a triplet rhythm or jazz swing feel.

To do this, we commence with a study of eighth note triplets and the way in which they are counted (refer to page 7).

e.g.: Count 1 + a 2 + a 3 + a 4 + a

We will refer to this as "Key Number Two".

You are now counting three even beats over each beat of the pulse, instead of two even beats. The rhythm of the syncopation will be played in a different position in the bar.

To analyse a bar of syncopation played as a jazz or swing feel, place it under "Key Number Two" thus:

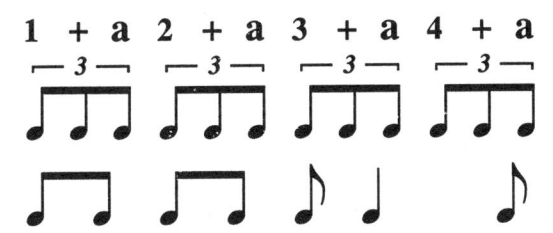

Then play the bass drum on all the numbers. As a time keeper, count "**1+a, 2+a, 3+a, 4+a**", and play the bar of syncopation.

A study of the examples below, will help clarify this method.

Example One:

Example Two:

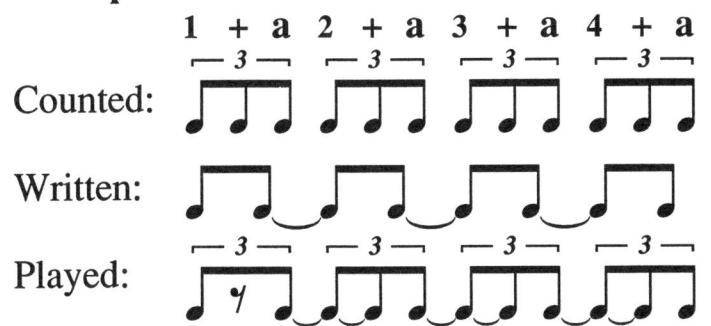

Example Three:

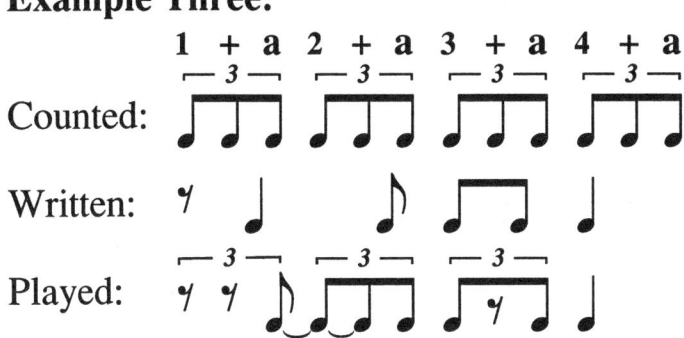

Example Four:

32 Bar Solo Exercise

Play slowly - count aloud - alternate sticking.

32 Bar Solo Exercise

Play slowly - count aloud - alternate sticking.

32 Bar Solo Exercise

Play slowly - count aloud - alternate sticking.

32 Bar Solo Exercise

Play slowly - count aloud - alternate sticking.

Lesson 22
Bass Drum Control for Basic Rhythms

The most common problem with beginners is co-ordination of the feet. When playing basic rhythms, it is essential to have reliable foot control. Make your hands fit in with the bass drum, not vice versa. The bass drum is the time – the pulse. It does not slow down or speed up according to the rhythm being played with your hands, it stays constant and steady. With regular practice, you come to *rely* on the bass drum for steady time, which produces a comfortable feeling with the end result of a confident, steady rhythm when you play. As you gain experience, the time can be transferred from your feet to your body, and the regular pulse is "felt" rather than actually played. This enables the experienced drummer to play rhythms within the time with the feet also, thus creating "four way" independence with the limbs. The following exercises are specifically designed for bass drum control. For further studies in independence, refer to "Progressive Rock, Jazz & Funk Drumming".

Start Slowly

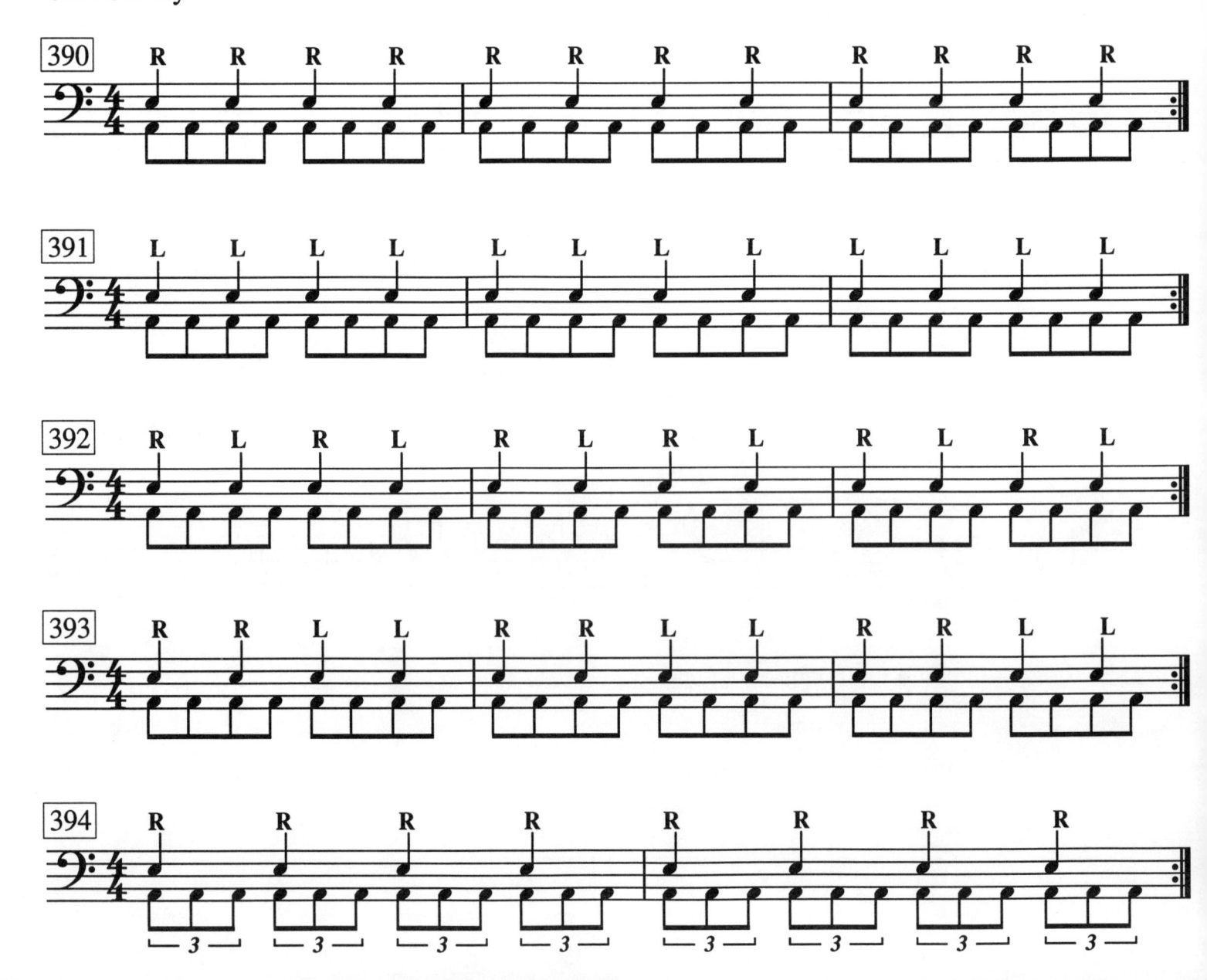

395
L L L L L L L L
3 3 3 3 3 3 3 3
396
R L R L R L R L
3 3 3 3 3 3 3 3
397
R R L L R R L L
3 3 3 3 3 3 3 3
398
R R R R R R R R
399
L L L L L L L L
400
R L R L R L R L
401
R R L L R R L L
402
R R R R R R R R
403
L L L L L L L L
404
R L R L R L R L

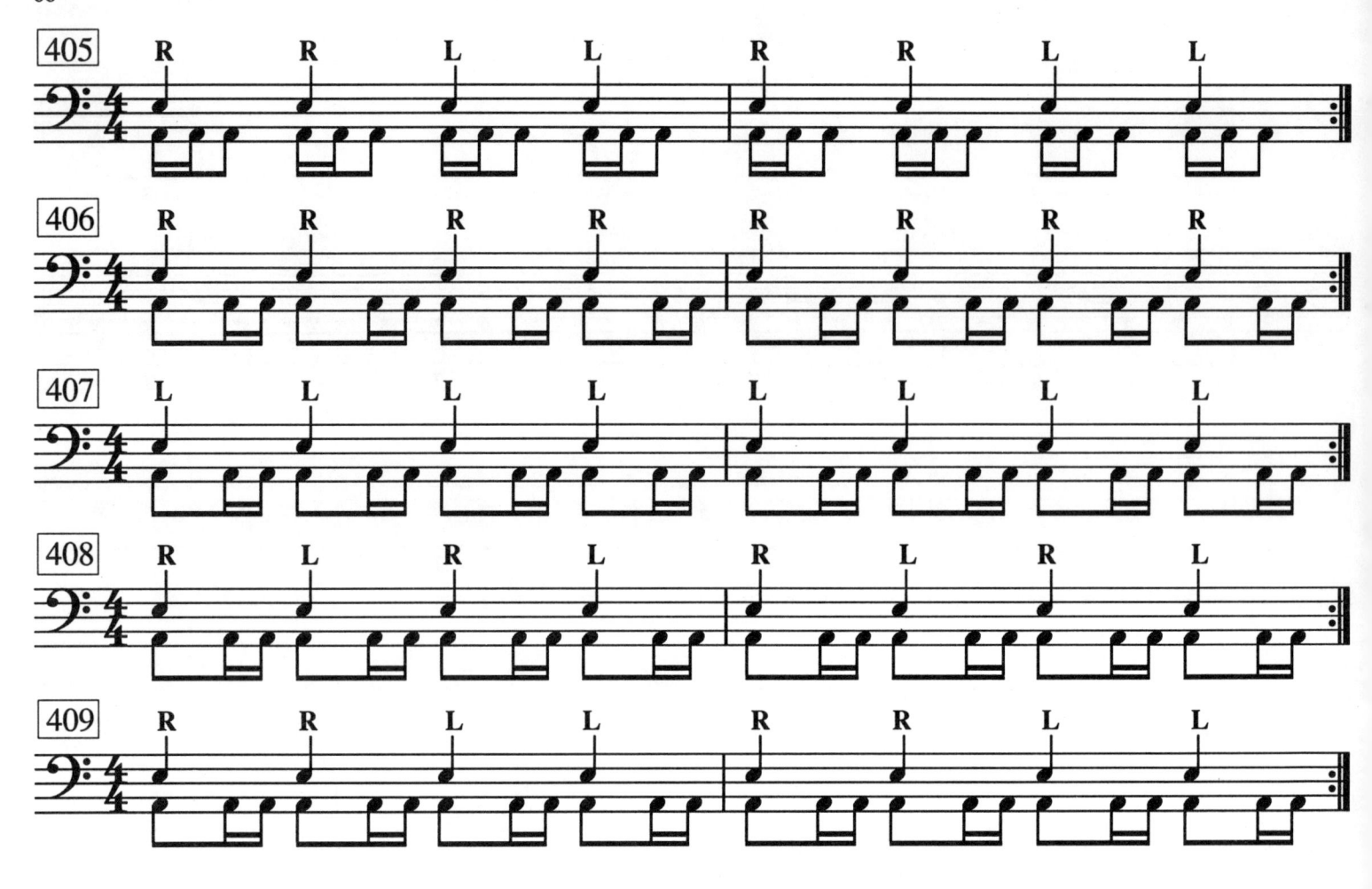

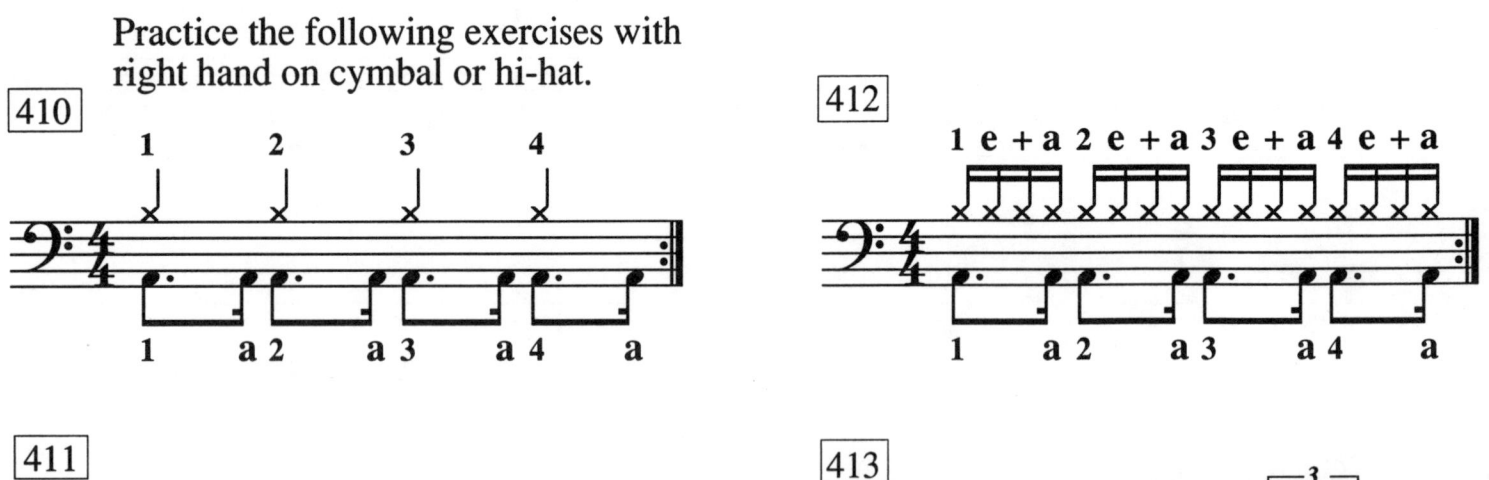

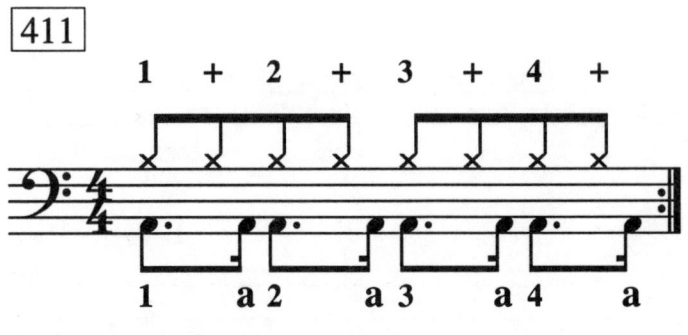

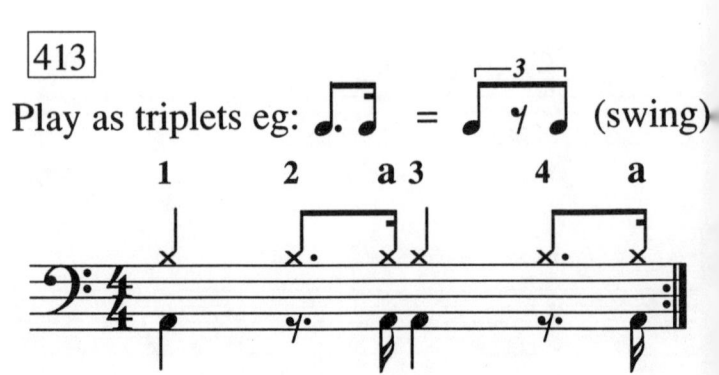

Practice the following exercises with right hand on cymbal or hi-hat.

413 Play as triplets eg: ♩. ♪ = ♪ 𝄽 ♪ (swing)